A Beginning-to-Read Book

A New School

by Mary Lindeen

NORWOOD HOUSE PRESS

DEAR CAREGIVER, The *Beginning to Read—Read and Discover* books provide emergent readers the opportunity to explore the world through nonfiction while building early reading skills. The text integrates both common sight words and content vocabulary. These key words are featured on lists provided at the back of the book to help your child expand his or her sight word recognition, which helps build reading fluency. The content words expand vocabulary and support comprehension.

Nonfiction text is any text that is factual. The Common Core State Standards call for an increase in the amount of informational text reading among students. The Standards aim to promote college and career readiness among students. Preparation for college and career endeavors requires proficiency in reading complex informational texts in a variety of content areas. You can help your child build a foundation by introducing nonfiction early. To further support the CCSS, you will find Reading Reinforcement activities at the back of the book that are aligned to these Standards.

Above all, the most important part of the reading experience is to have fun and enjoy it!
Sincerely,

Shannon Cannon, Ph.D.
Literacy Consultant

Norwood House Press
For more information about Norwood House Press please visit our website at www.norwoodhousepress.com or call 866-565-2900.
© 2022 Norwood House Press. Beginning-to-Read™ is a trademark of Norwood House Press. All rights reserved. No part of this book may be reproduced or utilized in any form or by any means without written permission from the publisher.

Editor: Judy Kentor Schmauss
Designer: Sara Radka

Photo Credits:
All images sourced from Getty Images.

Library of Congress Cataloging-in-Publication Data
Names: Lindeen, Mary, author.
Title: A new school / by Mary Lindeen.
Description: Chicago : Norwood House Press, 2022. | Series: A beginning-to-read book | Audience: Grades K-1 |
    Summary: "Describes what it's like to go to a new school, including what a new student might see and do there such as learning, playing, and meeting new friends. This title includes a note to caregivers, reading activities, and a word list. An early social and emotional book that includes reading activities and a word list"– Provided by publisher.
Identifiers: LCCN 2021049739 (print) | LCCN 2021049740 (ebook) | ISBN 9781684507863
    (hardcover) | ISBN 9781684047369 (paperback) | ISBN 9781684047405 (epub)
Subjects: LCSH: Schools–Juvenile literature. | First day of school–Juvenile literature.
Classification: LCC LB1556 .L549 2022 (print) | LCC LB1556 (ebook) | DDC 371–dc23/eng/20211106
LC record available at https://lccn.loc.gov/2021049739
LC ebook record available at https://lccn.loc.gov/2021049740

Hardcover ISBN: 978-1-68450-786-3
Paperback ISBN: 978-1-68404-736-9

347N—012022
Manufactured in the United States of America in North Mankato, Minnesota.

Good morning!

Today is your first day at your new school.

You have breakfast.

You get your backpack and your lunch.

You are ready to go!

5

You might walk to school.

You might ride a bus.

Or you might go by car.

Look at all these kids.

They go to your school, too.

Your teacher is happy to see you.

He has planned a busy day.

First, put away your things.

You can use the hooks and bins.

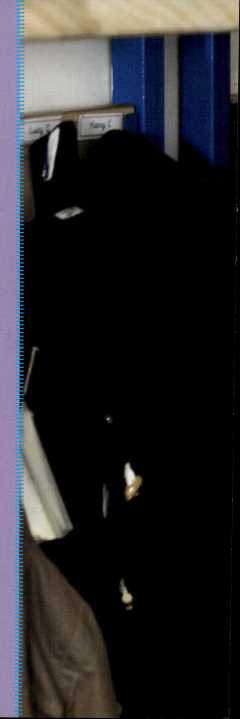

You might talk about the calendar.

Then you might do some math.

Now it's time for lunch.

You sit with your new friends.

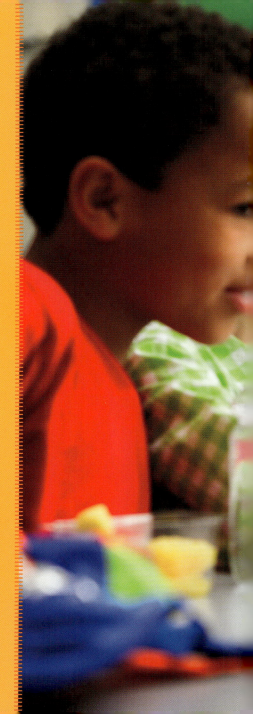

And now it's time to play!

Recess is over.

Your teacher reads a story.

All of you sit on the big rug.

Do you like to paint?

You can do that in art class.

Do you want to take a book home?

You can get one from the library.

Now the day is over.

You get ready to leave.

Welcome home!

How was your day?

Tell us all about your new school!

. . . READING REINFORCEMENT. . .

CRAFT AND STRUCTURE

To check your child's understanding of the organization of the book, recreate the following chart on a sheet of paper. Ask your child to complete the chart by writing the events that happen on a typical school day (add more spaces as needed):

VOCABULARY: Learning Content Words

Content words are words that are specific to a particular topic. All the content words in this book can be found on page 32. Use some or all of these content words to complete one or more of the following activities:

1. Help your child find the commonalities between the words.
2. Scramble the letters in the words and have your child unscramble them.
3. Ask 5W questions about the words: *Who? What? Where? When? Why?*
4. Have your child draw a picture to remind them of a word's meaning.
5. Make up riddles about the words.

FOUNDATIONAL SKILLS: Vowel Digraphs

A vowel digraph is two vowels that appear together but have one sound, like in *rain*. Have your child identify words with vowel digraphs in the list below. Then help your child find words with vowel digraphs in this book.

boat	fans	lamp
bread	heals	train

CLOSE READING OF INFORMATIONAL TEXT

Close reading helps children comprehend text. It includes reading a text, discussing it with others, and answering questions about it. Use these questions to discuss this book with your child:

1. What's exciting about going to a new school? Scary?
2. How might the girl on page 3 be feeling? Why do you think so?
3. How can a new school and an old school be the same? Different?
4. How could you help a new student feel welcome in your class?
5. What might the girl on page 28 tell her parents about her day?
6. Have you ever been a new person in a group? How did you feel?

FLUENCY

Fluency is the ability to read accurately with speed and expression. Help your child practice fluency by using one or more of the following activities:

1. Reread the book to your child at least two times while he or she uses a finger to track each word as it is read.
2. Read a line of the book, then reread it as your child reads along with you.
3. Ask your child to go back through the book and read the words he or she knows.
4. Have your child practice reading the book several times to improve accuracy, rate, and expression.

31

••• Word List •••

A New School uses the 92 words listed below. *High-frequency words* are those words that are used most often in the English language. They are sometimes referred to as *sight words* because children need to learn to recognize them automatically when they read. *Content words* are any words specific to a particular topic. Regular practice reading these words will enhance your child's ability to read with greater fluency and comprehension.

High-Frequency Words

a	first	is	put	things
about	for	like	read(s)	time
all	from	look	school	to
and	get	might	see	too
are	go	new	some	us
at	good	now	take	use
away	has	of	tell	want
big	have	on	that	was
by	he	one	the	with
can	home	or	then	you
day	how	over	these	your
do	in	play	they	

Content Words

art	calendar	kids	planned	talk
backpack	car	leave	ready	teacher
bins	class	library	recess	today
book	friends	lunch	ride	walk
breakfast	happy	math	rug	welcome
bus	hooks	morning	sit	
busy	it's	paint	story	

••• About the Author

Mary Lindeen is a writer, editor, parent, and former elementary school teacher. She has written more than 100 books for children and edited many more. She specializes in early literacy instruction and books for young readers, especially nonfiction.